Keeping Time:
Haibun for the Journey

Keeping Time:
Haibun for the Journey

Poems by

Penny Harter

© 2023 Penny Harter. All rights reserved.
This material may not be reproduced in any form, published,
reprinted, recorded, performed, broadcast,
rewritten or redistributed without
the explicit permission of Penny Harter.
All such actions are strictly prohibited by law.

Cover design by Shay Culligan
Cover image by Patrick Hendry
Author's photo by Penny Harter

ISBN: 978-1-63980-291-3

Kelsay Books
502 South 1040 East, A-119
American Fork, Utah 84003
Kelsaybooks.com

Preface

The first two-thirds of this collection contain haibun written before Covid arrived in our midst. I love writing haibun because of the interweaving texture of prose-poem and haiku, and I embrace the challenge of finding just the right haiku, inserting them where they fit best—haiku that do not continue the narrative but relate to it in theme or mood.

When I put together my newest collection of free-verse poetry born from those pandemic months, *Still-Water Days,* I chose not to include the many haibun I'd written, wanting to focus on my poems. But now I'm bringing together those haibun as well as many earlier ones that had not yet been collected in a book.

I've organized this collection as a calendar of days—first by seasons of the heart and then by the actual seasons. I hope you enjoy the journey.

Acknowledgments

Selected haibun in this collection have appeared in the following periodicals or anthologies.

Many also appeared on my Facebook page and are posted in my Blog on my website pennyharterpoet.com.

CHO (Contemporary Haibun Online): "Bird Watching," "Crow," "Harvest Home," "Requiem for the Bye-Lo Doll," "Tick-Tock," "Twilight Walk"

Exit 13: "Fishing in the Canyon"

Facebook: "Hefting an Apple"

Golden Triangle Haiku (2021): "all day long"

Grandmother's Pearls: "Pandemic Prayer"

Haibun: A Writer's Guide: "Driving Through the New Jersey Dusk"

Haibun Today: "White Stone"

Harpy Hybrid Review: "About Loss"

Keeping Time (trifold for HNA 2017): "Sycamore Time"

Lynx: "Keep," "Keeping," "Kept," "Portal"

Modern Haiku: "Driving Through the New Jersey Dusk"

One Hundred Gourds: "Bare Branches"

Prune Juice: "Relativity"

Rattle: "Night Howls"

Shrew: "For the Long Night"

Unsealing Our Secrets: "Among the Roses"

Verse-Virtual: "Keeping Time"

Visual-Verse: "The Arrival"

Contents

I

Portal	15
Bare Branches	16
Hefting an Apple	17
Harvest Home	18
Requiem for the Bye-Lo Doll	19
Dream Beds	20
Sleep Dance	21
Keep	22
Kept	23
Keeping	24
Blessing Dream, Santa Fe	25
Fishing in the Canyon	26
Restaurant, This Way	27
Driving Through the New Jersey Dusk	28
Twilight Walk	30
For the Long Night	31

II

The Way of Water	35
On a String	36
Night Howls	37
Among the Roses	38
The Arrival	39
White Stone	40
Glacier Time	41
Crow	42
The Cusp of Sleep	43
Bird Watching	45
Night-Fishing	46
The Known Earth	47
Tick-Tock	49

Relativity	51
Keeping Time	53

III

Pandemic Prayer	57
An Insistent Tide	58
Yesterday	59
Another Spring	60
Culling Clothes	61
A Thrifty Tradition	63
If I'd Had No . . .	65
Listening to Rain	66
Sycamore Time	67
About Loss	68
Today's Menu	69
Pitting the Alligator Pear	71
Fog Shrouded	72
Bird or Branch	73
Wild Lives	75
Testing the Waters	76
Learning to Swim	78
Evenings Like This	80
At Home in This Body	82
Husking Corn	83
Giving Back	84
October Riddles	86
Turkey Crossing	87
A Thing with Feathers	89
The Same Snow	90
The Hinge	91
Coat Pockets	92
Ghosting God	93
Indigo Journey	94
Searching for Omens	95

I

Portal

. . . a short passage to another room

Once a strange door hidden in a wall came out on wheels to divide one room from another. I don't remember that it closed off grandmother's dining room from the living, yet it does so now, emerging from its cavern like a fall of water between me and that table set with stone utensils on white linen—no, not stone, only seeming so as I reach through to lift them.

lost in the estate sale
that green glass globe
my mother loved

As we advance in any air, we enter something other, layers shimmering as we pass. Sometimes, strands will brush our cheeks as we move from here to there, from now to a time we don't remember—from one world to the next through the wormhole that awaits us.

buried in sand, my feet
emerge again—grains
falling one by one

Bare Branches

As I drive a snow-covered road through this old-growth forest, winding between towering trunks at twilight, I suddenly understand that the fretwork of bare branches is tree talk—the twists and turns of these limbs volitional as they stretch to greet one another or welcome the sky.

before the strike—
the owl's shadow
grows

We are together, the trees sign against the dusk. *We are one.* And when their limbs can't mingle above ground, their roots find one another.

family plot—
always room for one more
cremation

Hefting an Apple

At the farm stand by the orchard, the last apples of the morning light strikes the foremost baskets on the rough-hewn wooden stand. I heft an apple, feel how even in the sun it holds the cold of this February day, remember peel falling into the sink, scallops of seeds and core cut from each quarter, and the scent of baking pie.

mother's pastry brush—
stiff bristles bending
more each year

In the orchard crooked branches fret the cloudy sky. Snow is on the wind, several inches forecast for tonight. Late afternoon the farmer will put up chicken-wire around the three open sides, clear the shelves. As I prepare to drive away, he climbs back into his truck for shelter, chafes his chapped hands.

worn sleeping bag—
its red flannel lining
soft against my cheek

Harvest Home

country cemetery—
a flock of crows cawing
between gravestones

Last night I dreamed of climbing old stone steps, three tiers of them, like layers on a wedding cake, climbing to the top of a hill where great stone tables stretched out on a field beneath the autumn sky—each table waiting for a family to find themselves among the thousands milling up and down; waiting for some music in the open air as the tribes gathered round.

I stood on a folding chair and called my family in—the living and the dead—grandparents, parents, aunts and uncles, cousins, husbands, discarded in-laws, children, grown now with their own families—and they all came smiling to the feast, while behind them trailed the others, holding hands all the way back to wooden tables floating in the dust motes of long Thursday afternoons while the light waned.

acid-free paper
in great-grandmother's journal—
I reverse the telescope

Requiem for the Bye-Lo Doll

The fading shoebox on the shelf of my childhood closet holds the shattered porcelain head of my mother's Bye-Lo doll—a gift she gave me the Christmas I was ten. My excited hands lifted her out of the box, only to drop her onto the hard stones around the fireplace.

grandmother's attic—
sunlight breaking through
the dirty windowpane

I tried to sweep together the milky shards of her forehead, the curved and rosy fragments of her cheeks, the blue glass marbles of her eyes, while Mother, also on her hands and knees, cried.

after the fire
picking through the ashes
for old photos

I leave the shoebox coffin on its shelf, then study the backs of my hands. Blue-green veins swell as they fall from my wrists to my knuckles, and I am caught in yet another memory—my mother and I comparing hands when she was my age—her telling me that mine would be like hers, the bloodlines showing more with every year.

holiday dinner—
again my daughter asks me
to make the gravy

Dream Beds

Once I hung a dreamcatcher over my daughter's bed to trap the nightmares plaguing her. The next morning, I opened the window and shook it out. Redeemed monsters flapped into the trees, laughing.

dead wren under
the throw rug—small gift
from the grateful cat

My aging mother dreamed an angel's giant hand hovered above her bed, protecting her from harm. She could see it clear as day, she told us, and the next night her dead mother visited her.

stained glass window—
a rainbow shimmers on
the chapel pew

After the accident, on his deathbed Grandpa was young again, working with his brothers to restore a car. I kept vigil beside him, watching his hands at work, listening to his side of their conversation.

ear pressed against
the door, the child listens—
New Year's Eve

Sleep Dance

cave drawings—
ancient animals still
running in torch-light

We enter the bed, our movements practiced so often that they happen without thought. Your left arm splays out, inviting my head to snuggle on your shoulder, then wraps around to pull me close. My left hand begins to gently caress you as you stroke my back, our breath paced to the same rhythm—stomachs softly rising / falling.

Night settles around us, faint light from outside entering between blinds and sill. As we drift deeper, we turn to spoon on our left sides, the curves of our bodies fitting like pieces of a puzzle we've been working on all our lives. Taking a deep breath together, we let go.

Now we ride the waves of sleep—surfacing and going under, limbs sometimes twitching in dreams. Some nights we snore, wake to use the bathroom, then fall back into each other's embrace. Feeling too hot, too cold, our bodies sleep-dance apart and together, find new postures as we swim toward morning.

in his dream
the harmonica player
inhales a chord

Keep

~v. to be faithful to / not swerve; to preserve or maintain
n. British: pasture for grazing

We keep the hours, mark them on our walls, wear them on our wrists, hoard them in the chambers of our ticking hearts, faithful to the cycles we've ordained for sun and moon.

each year another
mark on the wall—
history

I keep your memory in cabinets of papers, on shelves of books, in drawings and photos, while the dust you've left behind has settled in a pillow that no longer keeps your head beside mine, though I embrace it nightly.

tide table—
the old fisherman
doesn't need to look

Kept

~v. tended, as in sheep or garden; watched over, defended from danger, harm, or loss

I have seen sheep—wandering white puffs glimmering in hillside pastures—though I have never tended them. My mother kept a garden, spoke to the earth with veined hands, raised smiling pansies. Years ago, I tended vegetables, worked to stir good topsoil into clay. Pole beans, squash, and ripe tomatoes tutored me in rhythm.

morning rain—
worms float up
from the dark

I have watched over husbands, parents, children, and dear friends, kept dogs and cats, and would defend from any harm those whom I love. But what of dangers that brook no defenses, losses that outrace the wind?

after the storm
an old hornets' nest
for compost

Our words, a flimsy hedge against their aim, may fail to hold them in restraint, may crumble in our mouths.

boundary wall—
every stone dug up
by human hands

Keeping

~v. restraining from divulging; withholding

I never told you that after you fell ill, I often woke in the night and turned to lightly touch your back, confirming breath. Or that I entered the child's room, leaned over the crib, and did the same, before I could sink into sleep.

spiderweb
on the windowsill—
the evening breeze

What else would I keep back from those I love? That when we wrap our arms around each other in the dark, we hold light—hug the flickering atoms that define our flesh? Or that our eyes have descended from stars?

meteor shower—
so fast, the dying
trails

I cannot withhold these gifts. And I will not conceal what I've prepared for our feast of celebration.

miso soup—
dried kelp unfurling
in the broth

Blessing Dream, Santa Fe

What animal gave me its ear last night, loved me enough to lick it deep into the hinge of my jaw? My fingers found it, softly furred at the rim, angled below my right temple. The ear was black inside, smelled of cinnamon and cloves, opened into a rocky den the wind scoured as we slept, the beast and I, on some mountainside.

on the horizon
veils against the blue—
desert thunderstorm

Awake now, I trace where the ear was grafted to my head, search the mirror. Morning rustles the cottonwood leaves outside my window, and I remember the black rattle that came before the ear, the gourd I have been running from, its furred wings still on the table, its sharp face waiting to sing.

pueblo dances—
the pulse of stamping feet
finds my own

Fishing in the Canyon

Between red rock walls that frame this canyon like hands tipped in prayer, the cerulean sky far above, a fisherman stands thigh-deep in the shallows, casting his line into sunlit rapids.

ancient dark—
brighter than the stars
cougar eyes

On the narrow road we drive up and out, sharp switchbacks challenging. Our laboring breath mingles with cool wind from distant ranges ablaze with golden aspens.

in the shadow
of the mountain, the far
canyon deepens

Dinosaur footprints on the cliff alongside the road, three-toed indentations on rock that once was sand alongside rushing waters. In petroglyphs scratched into the black scrim on the walls, prehistoric beasts are still running from the hunters' spears.

from abandoned cliff
dwellings, ravens call into
the past

We cross high plains of sagebrush and chamisa, the road an endless snake through sifting sands.

on the horizon
curtains of rain
filter sunset

In the dense dark, an elk crosses the road, stops for a moment to stare into our headlights, then slips into the brush.

desert lightning—
tumbleweeds scatter
before the storm

Restaurant, This Way

The small-town restaurant waits, its neon sign a signal in the dusk. Stainless knives, forks, and spoons, their finish dulled from everyday use, grace red plastic placements on the scarred wooden tables where a waitress lights the candles. Finished, she walks to the front windows, to search a darkening sky for the first star; she has not used up all her wishes yet.

country road—
following the taillights
of a distant car

From behind the swinging kitchen doors the scent of homemade chicken soup eddies around the old wooden chairs, their backs and seats curved to fit the human form. Chairs that remember generations of family dinners, the weight of booster seats for babies, and the occasional stranger, the one just passing through, who, hungry, and tired of plastic food, is lured off the highway by a hand-painted sign with an faded arrow underneath the words: *Restaurant, This Way.*

antique store
by the train tracks—
dust on the crystal

Driving Through the New Jersey Dusk

Bare trees stretch like avenues into this twilight's luminous green, and the stars draw near. The road unwinds past lit windows, blue silhouettes of bushes. Flickering headlights sweep toward me over the crest of a distant hill. The air I drive through smells of wood smoke.

Now a field begins, stretching its pale body under the full moon, and now the closed, black ranks of forest. Atop the next rise an all-night diner blinks. A few truckers sleep in the lot. Inside, the knotty pine tables are lit by red candles; the waitress sponges a formica counter.

Across the valley a train whistles three times, like the syllables of a childhood name suddenly recalled, carrying with them an ache for something I rush toward this night, some landscape lost so long ago I can only guess its vague shape.

The road winds on. An abandoned gas station waits around the bend, blue phosphorus numerals lighting the clock above the calendar.

crumbling concrete—
an old pickup fills
with chill moonlight

And out there, that glow in the sky, some city slows down for the night, neon still pumping. Passing through it, lights blurring like streamers on a birthday party hat, I find myself in the dark again, climbing into foothills of the mountains.

The past is our only security. The child I was still runs in the fields, still plays in the woods, still sleeps in a room with a night light. She comforts me, tells me stories about who we are, reminding me of landscapes and people known without trying in that long day and long night. I listen for a while and thank her for the memories. I was lonely before she began.

But I must drive a far distance to somewhere she has never been. I warn her that we might not know where we are when we get there. And then I comfort her, reminding her of something she knows but I had forgotten: the journey is our destination—the lost landscape, the nostalgia that swells across these hills, motive enough to keep going.

from the mountain
only rivers, only clouds
on this moonlit map

Twilight Walk

The duck has twisted its head to bury its beak in soft back feathers. One dark eye, half open, shines in the twilight.

reading glasses on
she studies the map of
her aging hand

Beside the lake, the small red leaves of a hedge glow in the dusk like the rim of the sky in still water. Below the old stone bridge the water's black; a few pale leaves float by, dark spaces between them.

winter night—
bare branches host
the stars

Your father liked twilight walks you say, as you lean on the cold stone ledge, a hedge spray burning in your hand.

the silence
of snow on tombstones—
even your name buried

For the Long Night

At dusk a crow calls from a branch of the dead tree beside the tracks. I feel the coming dark in its harsh caw. On this Solstice Eve, I light candles for the four directions, contemplate the hiss of flame and melting wax. Honoring the Earth, breathing the sky, I close my eyes and lean into the night before I tilt toward fire.

the night wind blows
through bare branches—
I answer

II

The Way of Water

Remember those little waves slapping at the dock of the boathouse where once you caught a sunfish on a safety pin tied to a string, then threw the fish back? You knew a web of weeds lived beneath the water's gentle invitation—algaed fronds that snagged your legs as you dangled them over the edge, and you would not jump into the slime and silt that lay below.

summer dusk—
in the backyard shadows
hide-and-seek

Later in the cottage you found the memory of water ringing the bottom of a porcelain bowl on a table in the spare bedroom. Three tarantulas crouched in wait for you; their hairy legs, big as your small fingers, spanned the iron stains of what had been a small taste of the lake.

poison ivy beneath
the beach house—sharp
shell bits in the sand

Now that you are older, you think you are safe on the shore, but water stalks you, will swallow you whole if it can and spit you out again reborn, your cells a colony of thirst, determined to keep it alive.

stunted corn stalks—
dust devils rise from
the cracked dirt

On a String

A spider has dropped into my dream. I'm not afraid, for I've got her on a string which I am pinching just behind her elegant black body.

fashion show—
model after model strutting
in stilettos

The red hourglass she bears is draining time, but she's tethered to this string that dangles from my hand, suspended in some dream of her own that has her slowly rotating in space.

fallen tree trunk—
fungi thriving on the
many rings

Since sometime I must wake, I need another keeper for my dream, for if this spider wakes to crawl away into the dark that beckons her to bite, she will poison the world.

jellyfish tide—
angry bathers cursing
at the sea

Night Howls

When the drunk neighbor across the tracks beats his dog again, the primal howling jerks us from a dreamless sleep. Once I used binoculars to see what manner of man yells *Shut the fuck up!* at a dog.

after the fire—
an acrid stench haloes
the burnt trees

How convenient for this man to have a dog. How practiced they both are at it—the dog on a short chain cowering behind his doghouse, the man descending the back stairs with yet another chain wrapped around his fist.

repeated whistle
of the midnight freight—
headlight bearing down

Among the Roses

When I was a child I learned how to kill Japanese beetles, watched an old man move from bush to bush, flicking black spots off rose petals, knocking them into a rusty can half-filled with kerosene.

under the hedge
a cairn of dead leaves
for the baby mouse

Pudgy face lowered, glasses sliding down his sweat in that apartment yard, he raised his chalice bloom-to-bloom, intent on the struggle, the frantic paddling before he pushed them under.

another goldfish dull
on the linoleum—food flakes
drifting in the empty bowl

Help me find them, he asked my cousin and me, and we did, caught in the ritual of beetle death, the quick movement of fat fingers that also wanted to touch little girls as the roses ripened, their petals black and oily even now.

on the wicker table
in his bathroom, a used book
of magic spells

The Arrival

We had thought they would arrive in something metallic, something saucer-shaped or triangular. None of us suspected that the tattered shred of a wispy white parachute floating down from a cerulean sky would harbor any threat. It seemed harmless as a cobweb.

low tide—
a colony of jellyfish stranded
on the dunes

But when it settled down in the town square; when we rushed up to touch it, they detached themselves from its cloak, translucent as ghosts, and drifted out among us. And when they moved toward the mountains, all the children followed.

No music, no Pied Piper playing or Orpheus strumming his lute, yet our children left us, obedient to the cadence of a shimmering dance.

winter night—
from house to house
the rising wind

White Stone

I am stroking a smooth white stone found on some forgotten strand. Sloped like a bear skull, it eyes me from a rusty indentation in its side. Caressing it, my thumb finds a cub stretched out dead on the shore, having swum with his mother too far—broken ice, no seals, no land, bad storm—until drowning, he washed up here to lie on his side, mouth permanently open.

senior center—
a woman asks for more
canned fruitcup

Glacier Time

They are melting, releasing centuries, stream by stream, back into the sea. Soon, coasts will forget the sky.

long gone, the leaf-boats
I sailed down running gutters
of my childhood street

We are camped nearby, watching the run-off cross pages of print, tracing it on photographs snapped by a satellite that peers at the Earth below as if it were an Arctic tern trying to find its way home. Our fingers are dirty, the ink rubbing off on our skin, the terrain smudged by our sweat.

abandoned playground
on the lot by the candy store—
rust down the slide

Soon time will flow backward down those slopes of ice, releasing bubbles of air so pure we won't remember how to breathe it.

midnight croup—
a vigil beside the child's
oxygen tent

Crow

twilight rain—
sheltered in the trees
a murder of crows

The mute performance on the sidewalk across the street is a dance—some coming, some going, cheeks touching, a few kisses, and then the patting of shoulders, the careful hugs among women in black dresses, men in black pants, their suit jackets off, white shirts shining in this late September heat.

drumbeats on the wind—
the high school marching band
practicing again

I wonder what occasion fuels this ceremony on a sunlit afternoon—and then I remember the elderly woman who used to weed her flower beds, bending to tear out vines and messy volunteers, sometimes pausing to wipe sweat from her forehead with a gardening glove.

open window—
faint crying of the baby
with a heart defect

Last night I almost killed a moth, kicked at the thing that grazed my ankles until it rose to light on the sill—how fragile its powdered paisley wings, its one remaining antenna. I helped it out the window where I must go now, taking flight above that pantomime, my shining head thrown back, my harsh voice scraping a dirge.

traffic stopped—
a long chain of headlights
enters the graveyard

The Cusp of Sleep

antique hourglass—
sand still trickling through
the brittle neck

Some nights, my late husband could close his eyes and see a kaleidoscope of images flying by behind his eyelids. He'd narrate this movie to me, its colors swirling so fast he almost couldn't keep up with them as they flowed into one another like spilled paint. Or he'd describe strange places he'd never been, in this life anyway, as they bloomed, brief and luminous, before fading like ghosts as others rushed in to replace them.

I couldn't do that, though I tried. I saw whatever I conjured up in those moments on the cusp of sleep in my mind's eye—an evocative name for whatever in our brain conjures images.

A year before he died, he decided to use computer graphics to reproduce one persistent image he felt he had to capture, labored over it several days and nights until he'd gotten it just right—then, happy with what he'd achieved, printed it on heavy photo paper and carried it downtown to the art store to be framed in plain black metal. He brought it home to hang above his desk.

Against a black background of deep space, floated an oval galaxy of blue, green, aqua, rose and rust—reminiscent of those photos from the edge of the known universe—and centering this egg, a black spider-like creature stretched eight segmented legs and curling antennae in perfect geometric relation to the transparent oval of its thorax, which gathered a cloud of light from its brilliant galactic web.

After he died, I wondered whether that spider had spun its web to try to catch and kill the hungry tumor in the center of his chest—an alien that some months later carried him out there among the stars. Or whether that spider *was* the tumor.

I still have his creation, couldn't give it away to the thrift store, or toss it into the dumpster that caught so much of what I got rid of before my move to a much smaller space. Here, I've buried it face-down on a shelf in my bedroom closet. I don't need to see it to remember that oval riddle, that egg-shaped web whose strands of light reach out each night to haunt me in the dark.

exploring red, the child
finger-paints on butcher paper—
lunar eclipse, winter
constellations brighten
in its shadow

Bird Watching

A bird in the house or hearing an owl call means death. My daughter is afraid of birds in the house, runs to the nest of her room while her father and I trap a lost robin.

surfacing from
an anesthetic fog—
whose heartbeat?

When a child, my late husband saw a hawk take a grackle, then witnessed his father shoot the hawk as they came upon it perched on a fencepost and shredding feathers from its prey, the pile of down below a rising barrow to honor the dead. The shredded grackle joined the bloodied hawk, sinking into that feather bed.

How many origami doves should we fold to hang above the crib of the past? How many canaries let loose in the mine will die before we learn to evacuate the dark cave of apocalypse?

solar eclipse—
too many eyes scarred by
the nuclear corona

And now I retrieve a random headline: *Nine Rules for the Blackbird Watcher*. Blackbird watching is less common than songbird watching, though the grackles' speckled iridescence glitters among dusty leaves, and the red-winged ones startle us awake, flashing their scarlet breasts.

red canyon walls—
ancient handprints
echo our own

Night-Fishing

The old red pump at the Texaco station by the river is out of gas. It's a relic, apparently crossbred with a mailbox. Its heaven is the end of a ramp that opens into a sky haunted by echoes and black exhaust. The roar of revving motors and the stench of burning tires live on in cracked macadam.

bologna on white
and a bottle of beer—
summer afternoon

No fishermen come now to fill their rusting cans before they go night-fishing off that rotting pier. My father told tales of boyhood cat-fishing. Barefoot in the swamp with his coon-hound, he poled an old skiff along star-filled creeks, fried his catch in an iron skillet beside the railroad tracks, then sold it to travelers for pocket money.

after the fire
acrid smoke ghosts
the dead trees

The Known Earth

Used to be flat—any horizon a cliff over infinity. And then the revelations of circles, orbits, spheres upon spheres, stars and planets hurtling through the heavens like embers spitting from the constellation of a dying log, or insects spinning in the spirals of a tenuous web.

between slates
I hose down anthills—
iridescent soapsuds

Each winter my elderly neighbor's garden grew paper stars, orange and yellow pointy things mounted on sticks among dormant rose bushes, painstakingly traced and cut by her trembling hands. After her death they flamed fiercely above the snow.

another year
without a Valentine from
the boy she loves

When the dead breathe their last, the atoms they exhale surround the known Earth as it rotates in place around a black hole. The scent of my father's cigarette filled the car while I lay full-length on the back seat, staring at the moon riding with us along some forgotten highway. Smoke from his mouth was comforting, along with the hypnotic hum of the motor, the strobes of streetlights.

no map for
this journey—territory
off the grid

Show me the way to go home / I'm tired and I want to go to bed, we'd sing as my father flicked lit stub after stub out the window of the 1934 Chrysler sedan, Betsy-car. Along the roadside, they flickered like dying stars, leaving in our wake tinder for a field, torches for a forest, and finally wads of paper and shredded tobacco bleeding into sunrise.

old bifocal lens—
one scratch through both
top and bottom

Tick-Tock

When the psychic told me a man was asking about a clock, I knew it was my father, shoving his obsession in my face again, this time from the other side of now.

For years he'd harassed my mother into daily winding his table-top grandfather clock, taught her how to move its hands, even correct it by hand when it lost time. She suffered its quarter-hour whirr and clang for decades.

Dad told the story of how his red-necked father had bought it off a tinker to commemorate the day my father was born, and that it had damned well better stay in the family! After both my parents died, I had it shipped back from Texas and gave it to my daughter since there was no room for it in my inn.

I don't know what to do with it, my daughter says as she dusts its walnut shoulders. *My kids won't want it after I'm gone, but if I sell it now, Grandpa will haunt me.* It sits on the sideboard in her dining room, witnessing our holiday feasts laid out on white tablecloths and graced with my grandmother's heirloom silver.

The psychic said the man was pointing to a map of South Carolina, jabbing his finger into its swampy woods. When I was a child, Dad dragged us there to meet his relatives, coon-skin-capped elders emerging from the trees like wary deer, gathering around to spit watermelon seeds over the railing of the log cabin porch where Uncle Framp lived, vying who could spit the farthest. Reluctantly, I joined in—and won.

When I visit my daughter, I stare into the face of that old clock, see my own features staring back from its hinged circle of glass. I don't know whether I gave the tarnished key to her.

Insistent as ever, my father's words are ticking from the limb of a dead walnut tree.

still sticky with sap
that tree stump we cut
last spring

Relativity

A man found an old grandfather clock abandoned in the swamp behind his house. Its rootless, weathered body was slowly sinking through a mess of sour ferns into the mud. The man and his wife dragged it up into a corner of their yard where the ground had been filled in and was more solid. Standing it up, they wiped the muck off its base. The man looked at the sky and saw that autumn was coming soon. When the ground froze, the clock would certainly be safe. He tried to wind it with a pair of pliers, but it would not start. So he removed its hands and drilled a birdhouse hole into the center of its face. It could shelter the winter birds. And in the spring, they could nest in the rusting clockworks.

construction site—
empty windows frame
the evening sky

He carried the gold-plated hands into his house and placed them on the corner of his desk. Many an evening through the long winter months, he played with the hands, arranging different times on the dusty wood veneer. And every morning when he walked out into his yard to check on the clock, he was sad that no birds had sheltered in it.

after the garage sale
the family sundial still
on the driveway

One day he gazed out his window and noticed the grandfather clock leaning toward the swamp at a precarious angle. It wants to go home again, the man thought. He looked fondly around his study. He could understand such a leaning. So he went outside, carrying its gold hands. After he dropped them into the bird-hole, he pushed the clock over and helped it slide back down the greening slope.

turning the compost—
too many beetles flail
in the light

Keeping Time

Two hawks circle far above, afternoon sunlight gilding their wings as their shadows swiftly cross the road before me.

In red canyons of the West, ravens ride the thermals, their harsh calls dark as the storm clouds shadowing the ridges.

again that dream
of refuge in a cave
above the river

There is no other place but here where hawks still prey on the living, ravens descend on the dead, and the clock on the wall keeps time above a granite counter-top, its polished surface chilled by mountain winds.

A gas burner spurts blue, steam hisses from the kettle, and between my palms a cup of black tea deepens as my breath rises warm through the strata of the sky.

nursing, the baby
smiles—milk bubbling
from her lips

III

Pandemic Prayer

I sit on the ground with a circle of people I know but don't know, and feel moved to pray for two of them, an elderly father and his grown son. Somehow, I understand that all of us circled around our campfire of fear need to hear good words about these two men—that both they and we need to remember the best of who we are.

hard to write my father's obituary

Both prayers last long in dream-time as I struggle to remember every good thing each has been known for, hoping to translate years of memories into loving words.

When I drift toward waking as the morning sun sifts through my window blinds, I try to retain their names—if ever I have known them—maybe Dave and Tom? But names are gone.

Grasping the unraveling strands of my dream, I realize I haven't known who any of us are, and that I don't need to know. It is enough to pray for them. Enough to pray.

that chipped white vase
with a bluebird on each side—
was it my mother's?

An Insistent Tide

The water comes in, not a tsunami but an insistent tide that rolls through city streets, rises on every building. We climb a labyrinth of stairs and tiny rooms to the high cubby we know to be ours in that vertical community, hoping the tide will spare us. And as we watch out our allotted window, it recedes, leaving the trees a brighter green, the streets swept clean and glistening.

at the center
of the maze, a circle
of blue sky

Suddenly we are hungry and wind our way down to a lower floor where a deli is offering free sandwiches and pastry treats. We fill our hands, keeping some of each for ourselves, passing more out to the others crowding the counter, and there is enough for everyone.

fresh trout sizzling
in the cast-iron pan—
wind from the sea

And I wake, knowing that this is the second dawn I have dreamed a flood.

fog shrouds
the field's edge—
we keep walking

Yesterday

The parks have reopened in New Jersey. A short drive takes me to a nearby lake. Hoping to sit for a while in the sun, I choose a metal bench overlooking the sandy patch of shore. Once, I would have dared the short concrete slope from there to the water's edge, trusting a balance that my neuropathic feet no longer feel, even shedding my sandals to step into the ripples gently breaking on the shore.

childhood swing
on the old oak—I fly higher
and higher

Down there, a mother, her young son, and a leashed German Shepherd are lingering. The boy enters the water, submerges up to his neck when the wind picks up. He must be chilly but doesn't seem to mind as he paddles around.

An elderly couple arrives, holding hands. The dog barks at them as they lean on the fence between me and the lake. They also don't walk down the concrete pathway.

sudden cold—
I wrap my arms around
myself

Gray clouds cross the sun. A pair of mallards arrows in for a landing, their dark bodies quickly gone around the bend. I get up, turn away from the lake, carefully walk over weedy grass and pebbles back to the parking lot, and head home.

sunlight flickers
on red maple buds—green
leaf tips tomorrow

Another Spring

Back in the 80s, after my parents moved from New Jersey to Texas, buying a lot next to my sister for their new double-wide ranch home, my parents still called two of their three bedrooms by my and my sister's names.

soon to be scrap metal—
abandoned swing set

When my late husband Bill and I visited them, we slept in Penny's room while my sister's had become a storage room. In that room I found an old photograph album open to a page that held my grandmother—a baby lying on a fur rug in front of a fireplace. Several years later when my sister and I were cleaning out our parents' home, the album was missing. I still wonder where it went.

visiting the
lost-and-found bin
hoping to recover . . .

These days, it doesn't take much for me to tear up, sometimes prompted by something random and unexpected, or by the sudden, brief visitation of a memory. Perhaps this year of isolation has caused my emotional vulnerability—this year of strange nighttime dreams, of time sliding into a stream of days, and of my growing empathy with all who have suffered illness and loss. Yet even so, I find something good to celebrate each day! We are resilient, and there is hope.

spring light rides
this morning's wind—
high tide in the river

Culling Clothes

Day after day, I've been promising myself that I would get to sorting through my closets and drawers, culling clothes I no longer wear (since I don't go much of anywhere these days), discarding pieces I'll never have occasion to wear again, or those too small, too large. Today I have at it, filling five bags to take to the thrift shop—returning many of these clothes to their origins in thrift shops months or even years ago.

again in the garden
she wrestles with the roots
of resistant weeds

I don't need that many clothes, have been living for weeks now in shorts, capris, or jeans, with a handful of short or long-sleeved tops. I have decided not to resume leading the twice-weekly meetings of the spousal loss grief-support group—meetings which helped define my days of the week for eleven years until the pandemic shut them down. I no longer teach either full or part time. Poetry readings are currently virtual and far fewer than they used to be.

Each piece I contemplate before pulling it off the hanger startles me with memory. These long pandemic spring and summer days have been full of reminiscences, partly from the fact of being relatively sheltered at home, and partly from an increasing awareness of aging—of years left behind, lives left behind.

sorting photos
I find myself in a hall
of mirrors

Some I can't part with. The gorgeous velvet jacket my late husband surprised me with one Christmas, or the multi-colored hand-woven vest—both from our Santa Fe days, and both of which cost far too much for our modest budget then. The jacket leads to the memory of the first time I wore it—some Japan-related celebration in Manhattan that Bill had been invited to. I felt so elegant, so blessed.

old beach chair
fabric fraying, still kept
just in case

Clearing my closets and drawers of surfeit, of remnants of the past, opens my way to different ways of spending my days. I'll continue frequent rides on the back roads of south Jersey, looking for turtles and deer. I hope to keep writing more, spend more time with family and friends, and yes, resume the occasional visit to a thrift shop for the fun of hunting and gathering, but limiting my purchases to only those things that are absolutely irresistible.

crepe myrtle—
that unknown flowering tree
I suddenly name

A Thrifty Tradition

Thrift or resale shops have been a part of my life since my children were young. My daughter never lets me forget that I put her in a plaid jumpsuit with a lace collar in kindergarten. And once in those long ago days when I needed a new winter overcoat, I found a great men's camel-hair, cut it down to size, then put it back together using the old Singer sewing machine I inherited from my mother.

blowing the dust
off the old doll's face—
grandmother's attic

Fast-forward to trips to Texas to see my mother and sister after both have moved there. Always, we go to the area thrift shops. I can still see in my mind's eye the little dark cap of my mother's hair as she wanders through bric-a-brac while my sister and I check out the clothes. This fall when I go to Texas to visit my sister again, we will spend several days visiting resale shops, often holding things up to one another across the aisles calling, *Mother would have liked this one!*

gone in the estate sale
two small family paintings
I didn't recognize

And now my daughter has converted to occasional hunting and gathering in the local thrift store, and my granddaughter, at college, loves nothing more than to go "thrifting" with Grandma. She looks for vintage finds, loves creating her own distinctive style. She's delighted to learn that there's a Goodwill in her college town. I know one thing we'll do when I visit her at school.

years since I lost
my balloon-tire bike
with green fenders

Thrift shops have become so much a part of my life that I frequently dream about them, one in particular that I have looked forward to visiting more than a few nights. It's upstairs in an old house, has several rooms lit by stained glass chandeliers. One room has shelves and racks with clothes, another housewares and bric-a-brac. I keep hoping that one of these nights I'll meet my mother there.

weathered barn—
rusted tools abandoned near
the rough-hewn cradle

If I'd Had No . . .

If I'd had no husbands, I would not have spent years sitting in a grief support group, counseling the abandoned. Each of us there had lost a spouse, each to a different wind, and some had no children.

What do we do with the nights? they asked. *The nights are so lonely, like empty shoes on the closet floor we can't get rid of yet.*

If I'd had no children, I'd raise my fingers to my lips and whistle another wind to carry me away to where they might be still waiting.

thrift shop rack—
bending to hear each
garment's whispers

Listening to Rain

Tropical storm Fay just swept up the East Coast, briefly pummeling the community where I live, about one-half hour inland from the Atlantic Ocean on winding country roads.

I return again and again to my front door, lean out into the windswept torrents of rain from the tropical storm that is grazing my area. It isn't forecast to cause serious damage inland, may just blow over some trash cans. Farther to the east, however, roads in the Jersey shore communities are under a flood warning.

after the deluge
digging fossil-stones from
the clay riverbank

I live on a busy two-lane highway. To listen to the rain I step outside and wait for a break in the steady hiss of cars, hoping to glean enough silence to spirit me back to former rain-blessed days.

rain streaks
the windowpane—so many
passing years

Sometimes rain is a lullaby. On camping trips when my children were little, I loved to tuck them in to the rhythm of rain pelting the roof of our camper, often fell asleep alongside them.

skimming the water
in the baptism font—the pastor's
practiced hand

My late husband once spontaneously said to me, *Once one has gone, how will we know we have loved? Raindrops will still run together on the glass.*

I listen to the rain.

Sycamore Time

When I moved into a condo in south Jersey after my husband died, I felt welcomed by the huge, old sycamore that graced the yard. Shading my new front windows, it echoed memories of the venerable sycamore that blessed the yard of the house we shared—its gracious canopy of shade and the endless drifts of leaves that we raked and raked into roadside heaps.

empty fireplace—
adding log after log
this long night

But over the twelve years I've lived here, I've watched my new tree slowly die—clutches of leaves shriveling, a huge branch let go here, another there. Finally management took it down, leaving only a sawdust circle in the grass, now grown over. Although I miss it, I welcome the sky.

losing count
of the boxes I haul
to the dumpster

About Loss

Recycled loss composts this garden. Loss of everything dear you've treasured since childhood: your tin shovel the sandbox swallowed. The mewing kitten your mother rescued from the white line. The dog a car found. The feel of your grandmother's hair and that silver bracelet she gave you that your little sister pulled from your wrist when you saved her from drowning in a big wave. The kite that flew away to Neverland. And that's just the beginning.

first look
through the wrong end
of the telescope

Look at the strata in that wall of rock? What got lost there? Floods and earthquakes, and the dinosaur whose footprints wander still, trapped for rockternity.

So what is growing in that composting soil, watered by the futile tears you've shed over the years as treasured things and even loved ones have gone under? Your wrinkled hands are still here, still able to grasp and let go. Sift that soil, let it dribble through the spaces between your fingers, raise it to the blessing of your breath.

after the party
a flock of helium balloons
in the backyard trees

Your father's gold pocket watch has been sprouting hands all over the place. Grab a few and learn the art of transformation. All your losses have recycled into dirt, and from that dirt a springing forth will rise, persistent like perennial bulbs that push up to reveal themselves again and again in all their transient beauty.

Today's Menu

Preparing the cup of coffee that leads off my day—one of just two cups, the second only half-decaf—has become a ritual. I observe each step of making it as if someone else's hands were spooning the honey into the bottom of the white mug with a blue crab on it, placing the paper K-cup into the Keurig machine, pressing first the heat button, then the one for cup size.

Thankfully, I can still hear the thin stream of water trickling into the cup, clearly see the cream swirl into the dark contents as I tilt my wrist to pour it, and savor the hearty flavor of my first sip.

Sometimes this is enough. I don't really want food most mornings. Meals have become too routine during these repetitive days—especially breakfast. Will it be eggs and gluten-free toast, or eggs on gluten-free toast? Should I butter the toast or not? Do I want to bother with oatmeal? Cold cereal gets soggy. Pancakes—well, that's more work, although I do enjoy adding a cup of frozen blueberries and stirring the batter to indigo.

remember all the hungry
children, Nana said—forcing
bite after bite

When my late husband and I visited my mother in her mid-eighties, each morning we would join her in the kitchen and ask how she was. As she padded around in robe and slippers, squeezing fresh orange juice and making the required Wheatena for my dad, her answer was always the same: *As good as can be expected.*

I remind myself of that as I embrace my morning. Write about what you know, they tell us. But some of these mornings I know less and less, and this is one of them. I take my coffee, move to sit by the window, and sip by sip contemplate the dawning sky, waiting.

stuffing my freezer—what is it
I am hoarding?

Pitting the Alligator Pear

First, select the softest avocado, not one so mushy you know its flesh will be brown inside, but one that yields to gentle pressure.

another how-to site
with a short video—true
or false?

Wash to prevent bacteria from transferring and carve all the way around through the leathery rind. Twist to separate the two halves, leaving the whole pit in to better preserve the half you won't be using. Then peel, slice, and enjoy.

a perfect peach—
ripe enough to just pull off
the rosy skin

However, if the pit easily splits as you slice, revealing its furry dark edges, its hollowed-out center, it's on its way to rot. When you cut around each half-pit to pry it out, don't cut yourself. Seeds hide secrets we usually can't see, some holding promises of growth, others of decay.

if you see something
say something—may we all
see clearly

Fog Shrouded

Today was hot and humid here in southern New Jersey, the air hinting of possible thunderstorms pre-dawn. I'm reminded of the opening words of an old English madrigal from the 1200s, one I enjoyed singing in an a-cappella madrigal group years ago.

Sumer Is icumen in—Summer is coming in
lhu-de ing cuc-cu—Loud sing cuckoo

Somehow we must be able to sing summer in these hard days, even when so much of the world is aflame with violence, consumed with grief.

in the distance
a child cries—smoke
on the wind

It's hard to find a song inside us when we grieve, or when our fists clench in anger. Sirens blare from the television in the living room, screams echo, car horns blare. I've never heard a cuckoo sing. But a year ago May when I woke to a foggy morning—

fog shrouded—
this morning's robin sings
inside me

Bird or Branch

Again yesterday, a drive out to the salt meadows. There in a small pond two mallards paddle in tandem, the male's plumage brilliant in the afternoon sun, the female's muted. He repeatedly upends, his beak probing underwater grasses as she floats serenely beside him.

long ago beach—
someone's tracing hearts
into wet sand

Closer to the road, something is poking its head just above the water. A kind of snake or frog? No, it's a pointed, stumpy jut of wood. Darkened by time, it lives there.

I want it to be an unknown—a new and mysterious pond-visitor like the large black bird sharing a bare branch with a smaller red-winged one. At first it looks crow, but from its open beak comes a repeated shrick-shrick clicking sound—nothing I've ever heard from a crow.

midnight waking
to almost-human cries—
mating raccoons

These lockdown days I crave the unfamiliar—something new and nonthreatening, yet mysterious enough to disturb my daily doldrums, excite my senses.

That piece of tree jutting up from the pond tells me that we are all rooted in one pond or another, parting the ripples we find ourselves in as a breeze pushes them. Here, the ducks' webbed feet contribute to those ripples, as do the sudden circles pinging the surface, probably caused by skimming insects or the brief risings of fish.

Trees group together yet make room for one another, forming families, communities. That dark piece of pond-wood has had to find a new family. I doubt it is conscious of the change, but who knows? Maybe every living thing is sentient, all of us interconnected members of the larger family we call Earth. And perhaps that is enough.

lengthening light—
a white ibis flies into
the dawn

Wild Lives

On the shady road into the marsh turtle-crossing signs cause me to scan the roadside. I'm sad to see flattened turtles who didn't make it and irrationally angry at the clever crows perched on low branches, just waiting to jump down and gobble up new turtle eggs even before the female turtle is finished digging her sandy hollow to receive them.

among the farms
too many *For Sale* signs—
shriveling corn

Emerging in front of me to leap across the road from a patch of woods between huge houses set far back among tall pines, first one deer, then another three, are here and gone so quickly into the underbrush my eyes can't follow them. I'm glad I am driving slowly enough to stop in time.

no need for
binoculars—I embrace
the horizon

Now a hawk spreads its huge dark wings above the hood of my car, arrows its body to hide among the dense branches of a towering oak, while in a neighboring field three wild turkeys strut their stuff, heads bobbing atop their red necks.

lost and found—
have we outgrown
the game?

How brief the flickering moments of attention we give these kin with whom we share our space before resuming our own busy lives. How transient, and yet . . .

birthday cake—still
able to blow out the candles
with one breath

Testing the Waters

Though it is more than seventy years ago, a clear stream still ripples over shining pebbles. Pillows of green moss line its banks. Holding my hand, my great-aunt Allie tests the shallow waters with her bare feet. I stare at them, pale and veined, daring the cold.

Up the hill the old white house and its green lawn await us, croquet wickets firmly planted, the worn striped mallets and balls poised for action in their upright wicker stand.

I am the great-niece, a little girl here with family to celebrate the annual July 4th birthday of my great-aunt Molly, Aunt Allie's sister. And we also celebrate my own mother's birthday which comes a few weeks later. Both of my great-aunts are my dead Nanna's half-sisters—Aunt Molly, a widow, and Aunt Allie a maiden-aunt whose fiancé was killed in the Great War. I don't know much about the Great War.

country road—
newly greening trees
arch over us

There are cupcakes with red, white, and blue icing, streamers to blow out, crepe-paper party hats, and sparklers for the holiday. After the birthday party, we trudge up a long green slope to enter the annual game of croquet, hitting our wooden balls until they roll through wickets into the lengthening shade cast by the house and tall trees. Down by the stream, two shadowy deer have come to drink at dusk.

Soon we go inside to gather around the old player piano and sing from worn songbooks the well-loved songs like *Down in the Valley, Sweet and Low,* and *Now the Day is Ending.* And then for my family and me, the day does end with a long ride home through the dark, my little sister and I asleep in the back seat of our 1934 black Chrysler sedan, Betsy-Car.

On the cusp of this year's Summer Solstice, the long light slowly fading behind the trees, deer still come down to drink from that stream. I test its chill waters with bare feet.

a distant dog
barks into the night—
and then another

Learning to Swim

my feet sinking
deeper into wallows—
retreating tide

I was eleven or twelve the summer after my Nana died, when the whole family went for a week to my great-aunt and uncle's old cottage on Raccoon Island, Lake Hopatcong, New Jersey.

I remember little of that time now, only the flashes that childhood memory stores in its pockets:

The boat ride to the island when I dropped Nana's pink plastic bathroom-cup overboard, and my Poppy cried. And the place Poppy set for Nana every meal while talking to her as if she were there.

The hairy black spider big as my hand nesting in a porcelain bowl on my bedside table.

All of us rocking on the old, screened porch overlooking the lake as the sun set.

The shadowed boathouse with damp boards rimming the edge where I sat, feet lapped by dark ripples, lowered a safety pin on a string, and caught a small fish.

And the small, rocky lake-filled depression at the shore's edge, just large and deep enough for a child to learn to float, tread water, and doggy-paddle.

The lost pink drinking cup, the enormous spider, and that first-caught fish have surfaced in the nets of other poems, lost now in former books. I've been learning to swim ever since, catching what I can as it floats by before I throw it back.

autumn dusk—
following vees of geese
until they're gone

Evenings Like This

It's early September, summer heat and humidity still with us from late August. Memories swirl on the slight breath of wind that promises rain—maybe some later tonight, certainly more for much of tomorrow. Too much has already fallen today over half the country, causing terrible flash flooding many places. And off-scale heat haunts California! A friend just fried eggs on the pavement.

Evenings like this I also pay attention to the climate within. Last night strange visions blew through my dreams, bringing me people and places I didn't recognize. And this twilight, the sky darkening a few minutes earlier than yesterday, I'm haunted by a harvest of memories.

another ride
through a moonless night—
ghost train

Fragmentary glimpses rise—long ago letting go of a kite over the ocean; plucking tomatoes hot on their stems in the tangled garden; the incessant harsh mating songs of cicada; my teenage arm drifting out the open car window to welcome the cool air of dusk after a day of summer work.

And suddenly I see my granddaughter as a baby again, sitting in her highchair. She happily waves the cookie she's gummed a half-circle out of, chortling one of her first words: *moon*. And now my toddler grandson, who started college this week, is lining up his tiny cars on the rug. Even my daughter's a child again, patting down sandcastles on Cape Cod, and my young son is drawing elaborate highway networks and jug-handles on white paper spread across the living room floor.

crayoning red
around my spread fingers—
whose hand?

Faces of loved ones now gone float like balloons on strings tethered to my mind and heart. They bob in front of me as I say my prayers and go to sleep.

The Almanac promises a cold and snowy winter here in the Northeast. I close my eyes to feel the flakes already falling, torn bits of lost postcards swirling past my windows.

It's gotten even darker out there. I stare at the white page of my computer screen as if it were a canvas, my words splatters of paint. Rain tomorrow, rain rain rain! And then clearing as a cold front visits us for a few days. A green wall on the radar is moving closer every moment. Rain's like that, here and gone, and here again. And I am here again. Still here.

At Home in This Body

I'm at home in this body where once an entire landscape flourished, verdant hills and valleys, rivers to be forded, mountains fearlessly climbed. At home in this body where once flights of stairs, like the bleachers in the football stadium during college, could be raced up two at a time. Where youthful passions flared, pregnancies swelled and delivered two babies, breasts gave ready milk. Slim and energetic, this body boded no betrayal, did not ache upon awakening or fear illness, another fall.

Still at home in this body, the landscape narrowed to what's possible these later years, I celebrate what is: survival after cancer and chemotherapy, after the new hip, after profound loss yet continuance, although some mornings like now, when the dream door cracks open to remind me of what was, I wake to sit on the edge of the bed, rocking my way back into now—this home.

another morning—
my arms rise like wings
in this autumn light

Husking Corn

Since I spend much time in the kitchen these days, I find myself contemplating simple tasks like peeling and coring an apple, cutting up chicken for soup, cracking an egg into a pan, observing the mysteries of pouring milk, frying fish. And now this revelation—husking corn. I do not take corn for granted.

rainy morning—
waking to the scent
of crockpot stew

One by one, I rip the green leaves off each ear of late corn in this bundle I got at the farm market. I twist off the tuft of silk that graces each tip, noticing how it stubbornly clings to my fingers and to the pearly kernels finally exposed. I rub it off under running water, remembering strands of webs strung between bushes that stuck to my face as I ran through them as a child.

traces of gossamer—
your fingers across my
aging cheek

The sink fills with corn husks. My late husband used to lay a few in the pot where we boiled the corn, not sure why. I gather them up and dump them into the garbage under the sink. If I had a garden I'd compost them, but there are no vegetable gardens in my condo development.

Here in south Jersey there are many cornfields. The stalks have all dried out by now, gone to autumn rust. Some days I, too, am rusting, or I feel husked, by the pandemic days, weeks, and months that have been stripping the leaves protecting my core. And yet, this harvest.

Giving Back

Yesterday, the trees in the graveyard had overnight gone to deep orange, rows of them flaming between the aisles of gravestones. I drive by this cemetery often, wait every autumn during the eleven years I've lived here for the forerunner, the one that turns first, now bereft of leaves, and then all the rest. What can I give back to these celebrants of autumn, harbingers of colder days to come when soon they, too, will be stripped to bare limbs?

unpinning grandmother's
laundry from the clothesline—
the creaking pulley

This morning, searching online for information about my great-great-grandparents, both fine nineteenth century artists, he of landscape and she of still life, I find a photo of a weathered gravestone, the kind that lay flat in the ground. Overgrown with lichen and moss, the name is hardly visible. My name is already chiseled into the small stone I placed over my late husband's grave in a cemetery far north from where I live now. The only thing missing is my end date.

not knowing then
what I know now—
the night wind

Last night I dreamed of teaching a junior high writing class, asking twenty-five students to write about three things that mean the most to them, perhaps even define who they are.

Immediately they begin to write. Afternoon rays of sunlight slanting through the large classroom windows illuminate them. I wake before I can invite them to share what they've found.

But as I wake, I remember my three choices: love of family and friends; my gratitude for being a poet; and my love of the natural world—all of which open my heart to faith and hope.

all day long, this
message from the sky—
sun clouds sun

By naming them, along with the further journey they have taken me on this morning, I now give back to those glorious trees among the graves.

As we face this coming winter, let us remember to celebrate what means the most to us despite this seemingly endless pandemic. And may we inspire others to do the same.

lingering sweetness
of apples in the empty dish—
savoring the crumbs

October Riddles

once again I fail
to accurately count the beans
in a large glass jar

Kick through the growing drifts of fallen leaves to separate the red from the yellow. How many of each?

If two clouds are drifting in different directions, which one will get there first? Multiply the time of day by the speed of the wind for an accurate map. How many spinning weathervanes know the answer?

elementary, those
pesky word problems
that haunt me still

Tally the clouds at sunset when they congregate on the horizon to sink into coral, purple, and finally dark smudges against the night sky.

How many drooping sunflowers in that farmer's field are going to seed under infinite stars?

Months of pandemic days have melted into lonely nights. What melted them? Will they fall off the edge of the Earth?

And so we go . . . but when and where?

distant whistles
of a freight train ride
the gusts of wind

Turkey Crossing

Two different flocks of wild turkeys scuttle across the country road, running from one patch of woods and field to another. A few are white with black stripes almost like zebras, others with feathers from brown to grey, black to rust.

Here and there, a hunter's empty pickup hugs the roadside. Most deer I'm seeing these autumn dusks are small ones, appear less afraid than their mothers who have probably been killed. This is also turkey-hunting season.

There are myths about white turkeys—some say they gave fire to Native Americans by shaking off their colored feathers, or that they gave us corn.

smoke-white turkey
fading into twilight mist—
litter of oak leaves

Here and there one bird is solo, but most move together, a community. Sometimes they congregate on the ample still-green lawn of a house set back in the woods. Deer do that, too. Perhaps they feel safer there than in the woods where the hunters are stalking.

construction paper
turkeys and pilgrim hats
on classroom windows

Remembered hymns echo in the chancel of my skull. I hum them as I ride between the autumn trees, many half bare already, into the country of night.

We gather together / to ask the Lord's blessing . . .

Come ye thankful people come / sing the song of harvest home . . .

Now the light's too dim to see deer or turkeys hiding in tangles of laurel and thorny shrubs, or lost among tall grass in rapidly darkening fields. But I know they are there, going about their nocturnal lives, and I give thanks.

this holiday season—
hard to count our blessings,
and yet . . .

A Thing with Feathers

after Emily Dickinson

Hawk feathers are used in ceremonial costumes both in Native American and Celtic rituals. They can represent hope, joy, moving toward a better time, can even bring messages from the spirit world.

grandmother's quilt—
tufts escaping from
frayed stitches

Today is my late husband's birthday. Since he so loved birds, shortly after his death twelve years ago, I laid a few feathers at the base of his photograph on the dresser, a hawk feather among them. Later I discarded the feathers since they were gathering dust.

downsizing—
what to let go of, what
to keep

While walking along a wooded road I find a clutch of brown and beige striated hawk feathers. No hawk lingers nearby as the source—the feathers are just there, a blessing in the roadside grass as if waiting for me. I pick them up, fan them out in my right hand.

low tide—
I gather shells
and their echoes

The Same Snow

All snow is the same snow, falling through the years that muffle the memories of caves dug out beneath the ice-crusts of childhood, or of hills that went on forever, offering breathtaking belly-rides on worn wooden sleds, flying from top to bottom—and then the long trudge back up, cheeks rosy and stinging in the cold.

again and again
we walk against the wind
on our way

We buckle our galoshes, pull on our snow-pants, zip up warm jackets, wind thick mufflers around our necks, and pull on the hand-knit hats and mittens that gather icy beads as we go. What distant slopes do we seek? What days and nights still swirl in the rising gusts that seize us?

snow angels
blow away—stardust
returning home

Now I open my window to both see and feel the snowfall thickening, the sky darkening as the planet spins into night. Thankfully, I have no need to travel, no need to risk icy roads or even walk out to the car. I am here, cocooned in my small snow-cave, grateful for the purity of white during this Covid dusk.

lowering a bucket
into the spring-fed well—
whose memory?

The Hinge

Snow and ice, ice and snow—a tsunami of storms crossed the country last week, cutting electricity, freezing folks to death in their homes, bursting water pipes, causing vehicles to slide into snowbanks, poles, trees, and one another, taking lives.

sleeping under
a single blanket—homeless
man and his dog

We ask the sky when this awful winter will end, when we can drop our Covid masks and breathe warmer air, celebrate snow melt sliding off our roofs.

This morning in southern New Jersey the sun has emerged again, although it's still cold. A flock of robins visits the wet grass out front, heads bobbing for worms. Later this week, days will grow warmer. We approach the hinge of spring, that time when the door swings back and forth, revealing each day's surprise.

sudden thaw—branches
from a makeshift shelter find
the forest floor

Some in the news predict normalcy by April, others by year's end. It will not be as it was, yet already there is more light.

purposely trotting through
alien landscape—red fox in
the breakdown lane

Coat Pockets

As late winter deepens, falling from a sky sometimes scoured blue, sometimes dull gray signifying snow, I dig out my down coat from the hall closet, stuff my hands deep into its pockets, and find the past.

Scrunched up tissues crumple memories, and crumbs caught in the seams must be the remains of last year's holiday cookies.

pre-dawn smoke
wakes me—which neighbor
still feeds a fire

This old coat no longer fits after months of indoor quarantine, and the top closet shelf is an unkempt stew of scarves, hats, and gloves.

Although we face a bitter cold, I welcome these days of lengthening light, hoping for a different spring, for a warming sun to finally unmask our weary faces and bless us.

again wishing
I were rinsing the garden
from my numb hands

Ghosting God

stained glass window—
all the saints orbiting
a many-petaled star

Multiple layers—waves and particles, solar winds, galactic light. Incarnating, breathing, searching hearts, sifting earth.

Ghosts visit a rabbit-ears TV: one potato, two potato, three potato, four. Difficult to find the singular in those grainy black and white days.

Iridescent slugs lay down slime trails on the slates of their lives. Ice glints in lakes and rivers.

Angels lie down side-by-side, their arced wings scraping through the snow to the grass beneath.

Let it all in—stinging cheeks, star-blind eyes.

Multiple layers—aurora on the horizon, always beyond reach.

thawing
the dead field mouse
opens its mouth

Indigo Journey

Toward morning, when dreams often rise from the depths of sleep, I dream a vast, almost indigo river, or maybe a fjord, and I am walking over this brilliance on a wooden footbridge with rope railings—walking out to a dock at the end to meet the small, open ferry that will carry me across to the far shore. I trust this bridge mounted on sturdy pilings and take my time, savoring the journey.

unpinning her hair
the elderly woman gives it
to an autumn wind

A shining expanse flows to my right, darkens a little under the shadows of the bridge slats, then continues to my left, curving around a bend as it finds the horizon. Reaching the dock, I scan the waters ahead of me, no ferry in sight. Just a vast body of blue. I know the ferry comes often to take travelers across that which cannot be bridged. But when I look behind me, no one else is queuing up for the ride.

carnival morning—
sun gilds the empty saddles
on the carousel

Somehow, though, that's just fine. I'm right where I ought to be, on the verge of waking, maybe even ready to gracefully dive off the dock and float with the current, wherever it takes me. I know I will not drown.

first time down
the playground slide—the toddler
trusts the landing

Searching for Omens

Migrating across time ravens have been omens, their raucous bodies dropping from the sky to finish the job on battlefields.

And their corvid cousins, the crows, have often brought grim tidings, their coarse caws announcing the death they carry under their wings.

For weeks I have been haunted by omens that witness these times, have seen these dark birds circling still.

inverting the toaster
I shake its burnt crumbs
into the sink

But I now search for other omens, ones that might bring hope in times of pestilence and war, of senseless slaughter, cruelty and greed.

So I look to the simplicity of this morning's sunlight, the scent of fresh coffee, the miracle of an apple I can slice and pair with cheddar cheese.

blooming again
in the neighbor's garden
a widow's rosebush

And as I break my nightly fast, I give thanks that I'm still here, having survived what we all must—my shares of sorrow, loss, illness, the turbulence of years.

Perhaps I am here for this—to love the broken world, affirming again and again that even on those days when the dark birds haunt us, we must seek sustenance in our daily bread and do whatever work we can to praise the light.

Tips for Writing Haibun

1. A haibun is not a short story. A haibun relates a journey, whether the travel is a physical exploration of the world or an internal journey of spiritual and/or emotional discovery. It should take the reader somewhere—from here to there.

2. Both the prose and haiku should be image-centered. Trim the language in the prose section to its essence. The prose portion can be written in sentence fragments or complete sentences.

3. The haibun prose should be more akin to a prose-poem. And rather than in paragraph format, the prose is usually presented in blocks. Some contemporary haibun are even in verse form with haiku indented before and between stanzas, or at the poem's end.

4. There is no set length to a haibun. It can be one paragraph with one haiku, or several pages with haiku interspersed throughout.

5. Many haibun are simply narratives of special moments in a person's life. Like haiku, haibun often begin in everyday events—minute particulars of object, person, place, and/or action.

6. Haibun are usually autobiographical and personal, and most often written in present tense.

7. However, some haibun published in contemporary journals also recount actual travels, memories, dreams, and fantasies.

8. The haibun's haiku do connect to the prose, but in the best haibun, the haiku do not directly continue the narrative. Instead, they relate in theme, mood, or tone. Inserting the haiku into the haibun is like throwing a stone into a pond—causing ripples of association.

About the Author

Penny Harter, co-author with her late husband William J. Higginson of *The Haiku Handbook,* is a past-president of the Haiku Society of America. Her work, both haiku-related and free verse, appears in numerous journals and anthologies. Among her many published books and chapbooks, six feature haiku and related genres.

Journals such as *Persimmon Tree, Rattle, Tattoo Highway, Tiferet,* and *Windhover* have published her work, and a poem of hers was featured in *American Life in Poetry.* Her newest collections of poems are *A Prayer the Body Makes* (2020) and *Still-Water Days* (2021), both from Kelsay Books. Other recent books include *The Resonance Around Us* (Mountains and Rivers Press); *One Bowl* (Snapshot Press); and *Recycling Starlight* (Mountains and Rivers Press).

A featured reader at the 2010 Geraldine R. Dodge Foundation Festival, Harter has received three poetry fellowships from the New Jersey State Council on the Arts, the Mary Carolyn Davies Award from the Poetry Society of America, a teaching-artist award from the Dodge Foundation, the William O. Douglas Nature Writing Award, and two residency fellowships from the Virginia Center for the Creative Arts.

Some haiku-related journals and anthologies featuring her work include *Haiku Moment; Journey to the Interior: American Versions of Haibun; Global Haiku; The Unswept Path; Modern Haibun and Tanka Prose;* and *Contemporary Haibun: Volume 12.* Her exercise for poets, "Circling the Pine: Haibun and the Spiral Web" appears in *Wingbeats: Exercises & Practice in Poetry* (2011).

She has attended, and often presented at, every Haiku North America conference but the first one. For more information, please visit her current website: pennyharterpoet.com.

www.ingramcontent.com/pod-product-compliance
Lightning Source LLC
Chambersburg PA
CBHW022016160426
43197CB00007B/458